· Véronique Enginger ·

The Magic of

# Christmas

## to Cross Stitch

French Charm for Your
Stitchwork

**SCHIFFER CRAFT**

4880 Lower Valley Road     Atglen, PA 19310

Originally published as *La magie de Noël à broder au point de croix* © 2016 by Mango, a subsidiary of Fleurus Éditions, Paris. Translated from the French by Omicron Language Solutions, LLC.

Library of Congress Control Number: 2017949952

Cover design by Molly Shields

Concept, patterns/illustrations, and instructions: Sylvie Blondeau
Photography: Fabrice Besse
Styling: Sonia Roy
Editorial director: Tatiana Delselle
Editor: Mélanie Jean
Artistic director: Chloé Eve
Typesetting: Élise Bonhomme
Production: Audrey Bord
With thanks to Mélissa Lagrange for her valuable help.

Type set in Honey Script/Archer/Thirsty Script/HipsterFontNormal

ISBN: 978-0-7643-5461-8
Printed in China
6 5 4 3

Published by Schiffer Craft
An imprint of Schiffer Publishing, Ltd.
4880 Lower Valley Road
Atglen, PA 19310
Phone: (610) 593-1777; Fax: (610) 593-2002
info@schifferbooks.com
www.schiffercraft.com

For our complete selection of fine books on this and related subjects, please visit our website at www.schifferbooks.com. You may also write for a free catalog.

Schiffer Publishing's titles are available at special discounts for bulk purchases for sales promotions or premiums. Special editions, including personalized covers, corporate imprints, and excerpts, can be created in large quantities for special needs. For more information, contact the publisher.

We are always looking for people to write books on new and related subjects. If you have an idea for a book, please contact us at proposals@schifferbooks.com.

Thanks to DMC for supplying the canvases used for the embroideries shown. www.dmc.com
Thank you to Marylise for suggesting this book project,
and to Mélanie for accompanying me through it. —Sylvie Blondeau

**Other Schiffer Books by the Author:**
*Retro Cross Stitch: 500 Patterns, French Charm for Your Stitchwork*, ISBN 978-0-7643-5479-3
*Fables & Fairy Tales to Cross Stitch: French Charm for Your Stitchwork*, ISBN 978-0-7643-5478-6

**Other Schiffer Books on Related Subjects:**
*Inspiration Kantha: Creative Stitchery and Quilting with Asia's Ancient Technique*, Anna Hergert, ISBN 978-0-7643-5357-4
*The Art of Weaving a Life: A Framework to Expand and Strengthen Your Personal Vision*, Susan Barrett Merrill, ISBN 978-0-7643-5264-5
*The Little Guide to Mastering Your Sewing Machine: All the Sewing Basics, Plus 15 Step-by-Step Projects*, Sylvie Blondeau, ISBN 978-0-7643-4970-6

Christmas! It's a time of expectation for small children, and, for those who want to make this holiday an exceptional moment, it's a time of effervescence. A time set apart, decorated in red and green, where twenty-four short days of December countdown contain children's dreams and the joy of preparations. Decorating, creating, offering, thinking of others—this is true Christmas magic. I hope that you will find ideas in this book to please you and your loved ones. Happy embroidering!

Véronique Enginger

The Projects

# Holly Wreath and Candies

December 1: The delicious countdown to Christmas has begun! You have to be patient for only another twenty-four days before the family feast and opening the long-awaited presents. Let the spirit of Christmas fill you by embroidering this holly wreath full of sweet things . . .

## Make a Christmas Wreath

Materials:
- A piece of supple cardboard
- Two different-sized bowls for tracing the circles
- A pair of scissors
- A pen
- Two sheets of different-colored paper (red and gold, for example)
- Transparent tape or a stapler

Place the larger bowl on the cardboard and trace a circle with the pen. Do the same with the smaller bowl, placed in the center of the first circle. Cut them out to make a wreath base.

Draw and cut out holly leaf shapes on the two pieces of paper. Roll up the ends of each leaf for a three-dimensional effect, and arrange them attractively on the wreath, attaching them with the transparent tape (or stapler). Don't hesitate to overlap the leaves to make a fuller wreath. Repeat the operation until you have completely covered the wreath.

# First Snowfall

Snowmen, sledding, and snowball fights . . . recapture your childhood with this design that features the gentle flavor of the first snowfall.

"Snow has the secret of restoring to the heart the childish delight the years have mercilessly snatched away."

—Antoine Maillet

# Toyshop Window

True works of art, the department stores' windows light up the long winter nights with their sparkling garlands and magical puppets. The bears, dolls, and other delights that make up this design will put stars into your eyes.

## THE SPARKLING STORY OF CHRISTMAS WINDOW DRESSING

Marveling at the department store holiday window displays is part of the magic of the season for many of us. Bright tiny lights, gift-wrapped boxes, and richly adorned Christmas trees catch the eye of shoppers of all ages.

The history of this tradition has roots in the late 1800s, when plate glass became widely available and store owners installed large floor-to-ceiling windows to attract passersby. Welcome to the world, window shopping!

One of the first major holiday window displays was put up by Macy's in New York, in 1874. When Lord & Taylor opened its flagship store on Fifth Avenue in 1914, it included hydraulic lifts under each of the store windows, so that staff could work on the window scenes out of public view in a sub-basement, and later the platform could be elevated to street level. In 1938, another first: Lord & Taylor unveiled a purely decorative display, no longer presenting store merchandise at all! The display featured bells that swung in sync with recorded sounds of sleigh bells.

As department store window displays have become more spectacular in their technical design, they remain amazing self-contained small theaters . . . enchanting universes that draw us in, adults and children alike!

# *Letter to Santa*

Dear Santa,

For a rich and creative year, we embroiderers wish to find original-colored skeins of floss under the Christmas tree!

While we wait for those marvelous colors, here is a charming design to stitch: children who are both impatient and full of hope.

## GETTING YOUR LETTER TO SANTA CLAUS

As everyone knows, there are many ways to let Santa know what you want for Christmas. The process has even been adapted to keep up with new technology. Today it's possible to send an e-mail to Santa or write to him on his Facebook page!

The use of the post office to contact St. Nick began shortly after the Civil War. Cartoonist Thomas Nast's illustrations were published in the widely read *Harper's Weekly*, and in 1879 he drew a boy using the US Mail to write to Santa, putting a letter addressed to "St. Claus, North Pole" in a mailbox.

In the years to come, so many letters to Santa piled up that by the turn of the twentieth century, the Post Office had fallen behind, and the public and the press began complaining about the situation. The process of answering Santa's letters has become more efficient, and in 2006 the Postmaster General formalized Operation Santa Claus nationally, putting in place a set of guidelines for all post offices taking part in the program.

# Santa's Sack

To help Father Christmas distribute his gifts,
make him a nice sack to keep all his things in!

*Instructions on page 90.*

# Saint Nicholas

The delicious smell of cookies fresh from the oven floats over this design. Embroider this tempting design and offer it, in the spirit of Saint Nicholas, to your family!

In the third century, St. Nicholas, the bishop of Myra (in modern-day Turkey), became known for giving gifts to poor children. In many households, his feast day, December 6, is an occasion for gifts.

## CHRISTMAS COOKIES

The earliest examples of Christmas cookies in the United States were brought by the Dutch in the early seventeenth century. Today the tradition of making cookies in Christmas shapes (tree, stars, snowflakes . . .) is an important event during the festive period. Often the entire family (or friends) takes part in making the cookies, in keeping with the spirit of Christmas. Sablés, the French version of sand tarts, serve the purpose perfectly.

## Christmas Sablés

**Preparation time:** 20 minutes
    + 2 hours for the dough to rest
**Baking time:** 10 minutes
**Yield:** 30 cookies

> 2 teaspoons ground cinnamon
>
> 1 star anise
>
> 3 cloves
>
> 1½ C sifted flour
>
> 2 egg yolks
>
> ½ C + 1 T butter, melted
>
> ⅔ C sugar
>
> 1 pinch of salt

Grind the star anise and the cloves. Sift the powdered spices into the cinnamon and sugar.

In a large bowl, beat the melted butter and the sugar mixture. Add the pinch of salt.

Beat in the egg yolks and then the flour. Gather the dough into a ball.

Wrap the dough in plastic wrap and leave it to rest in the fridge for two hours.

Preheat the oven to 350° F. Roll out the dough to a thickness of about ¼". Using cookie cutters, cut out Christmas shapes.

Place the cookies on a baking sheet lined with parchment paper. Bake for approximately 10 minutes, until the cookies are firm but not browned.

# Getting the Christmas Tree

Ah, sweet nostalgia, the smell of fresh pine awakens our best memories of Christmas, also captured in this wintertime design.

"Christmas is neither a time nor a season; it is a state of mind."
—President Calvin Coolidge

# Santa's Workshop

Christmas is coming and the elves are busy getting the toys finished in time to fill good old Santa's sack. Now it's your turn to reproduce all the good energy that comes from these charming little elves as they go about happily preparing.

## SANTA CLAUS VILLAGE

Santa Claus Village can be visited year round, but it's a not-to-be-missed destination when December rolls around. According to legend, Father Christmas lives in Lapland, and this is why the village was built on the Arctic Circle. Created in 1950, it's situated north of Rovaniemi, Finland.

After a ride in a sled pulled by reindeer or dogs, after a trip to Santa Claus's main post office, or after playing Lapp games, you can actually meet the famous and generous Santa in his red suit!

An interesting note: Eleanor Roosevelt was the village's first official tourist, in 1950. If you are lucky enough to visit Santa Claus country, you can see the "Mrs. Roosevelt Cabin," built in her honor.

# My Lovely Tree

Colorful baubles, a few strings of lights, and a star fixed to the topmost branch. It doesn't take much to make children smile in delight. Get your needles and floss ready and decorate this lovely tree design in your own way. You'll see—the good-mood effect is instantaneous.

### Oh Christmas Tree

Oh Christmas tree, oh Christmas tree,
How lovely are thy branches!
Oh Christmas tree, oh Christmas tree,
How lovely are thy branches!

Not only green when summer's here,
But also when it's cold and drear.
Oh Christmas tree, oh Christmas tree,
How lovely are thy branches!

Oh Christmas Tree, oh Christmas Tree,
What happiness befalls me
When oft at joyous Christmastime
Your form inspires my song and rhyme.
Oh Christmas Tree, oh Christmas Tree,
What happiness befalls me!

# Evergreen Wreaths

Beloved decorations for the end-of-the-year holidays, holly wreaths and mistletoe are honored in this design. Get out your best threads and embroider these symbols of happiness.

## TRADITIONAL KISSES
## UNDER THE MISTLETOE

Throughout the end-of-the-year festivities, there is a long-standing custom of stealing a kiss under the mistletoe. Where does this tradition come from? A sign of good luck and a long life, the ritual is rooted in diverse sources.

It was a symbol of immortality for the Celts (because mistletoe's leaves are always green, even in the winter), and exchanging a kiss under a branch of mistletoe was a sign of friendship and goodwill.

For the Anglo-Saxons, the custom was linked to the legend of Freya, goddess of love, beauty, and fertility. Even today, when lovers kiss under the mistletoe it is interpreted as a promise of marriage, but also of happiness, long life . . . and fertility!

# Christmas Tree Ornaments

It's such a pleasure to decorate the Christmas tree, especially when you've created the ornaments yourself!

*Instructions on page 91.*

# Reading Christmas Stories

Comfortably settled with their favorite toys, these two angel-faced children escape into the magic of Christmas fairy tales. Curled up in a soft blanket or beside a cheerful fire in the grate, let the magic of Christmas warm you stitch after stitch.

## THE BEST CHRISTMAS FAIRY TALES

Of all nights, Christmas Eve is the most magical for children. The sweet nostalgia of these hours has inspired numerous writers. Christmas has given birth to fairy tales that are mythical and charming.

Among them, of course, is the classic tale of *The Nutcracker and the Mouse King* by Ernst Theodor Amadeus Hoffmann, in which a nutcracker with a broken leg comes to life and protects young Marie from the diabolical Mouse King.

More tragically, "The Little Match Girl" by Hans Christian Andersen tells the story of a poor little girl who tries to sell matches to passersby to help feed her family. Barefoot in the snow, she tries to warm herself by lighting matches, but sadly she dies on New Year's Eve after seeing visions that warmed her heart.

Let's not forget Charles Dickens and his *A Christmas Carol*. Scrooge, a mean old man, chooses to spend Christmas on his own, but the Christmas Spirits decide otherwise and the old man is dragged to his past, his present, and his future to show him how he'll end up if he continues to pretend that happiness doesn't exist.

# Animals Celebrate Christmas

Aren't these charming animals adorable as they get ready to celebrate Christmas? These designs would make pretty napkins, for example, to enjoy on Christmas Eve.

## SANTA'S REINDEER

As famous as Father Christmas himself, the nine flying reindeer fascinated us when we were children, but can you remember the names of all of them? Here's a short reminder…

At the beginning there were eight reindeer: four males and four females. Their names are:

**Dasher:** the fastest

**Dancer:** the most graceful

**Prancer:** the most powerful

**Vixen:** strong and beautiful

**Comet:** who brings happiness to children

**Cupid:** who brings love to children

**Donner:** the loudest, like thunder

**Blitzen:** who brings light

A small reindeer was added in 1939: **Rudolph.**

He first appeared in a 1939 story by Robert L. May, a catalog writer for the now-defunct Montgomery Ward department stores, and Rudolph's special feature is that his nose is red and lights up. His nose helps him guide the sleigh and face terrible weather conditions that would otherwise risk making Santa late in delivering his presents.

# Caroling

In this scene we see crystal-clear-voiced and angelic-faced children singing the most-beautiful Christmas carols. On a canvas as white and pure as snow, reproduce this tableau where the nuances of blue conjure up winter mornings. Irving Berlin's 1942 song "White Christmas" captures our ideal memories, and its power has not dimmed in the past seventy-five years. The version sung by Bing Crosby is the world's bestselling single worldwide

### White Christmas

I'm dreaming of a white Christmas
Just like the ones I used to know
Where the treetops glisten
and children listen
To hear sleigh bells in the snow

I'm dreaming of a white Christmas
With every Christmas card I write
May your days be merry and bright
And may all your Christmases be white

# Christmas Decorations

Rich in color, delicate and sparkling, Christmas decorations give life to the frozen winter décor. For a 100 percent creative Christmas, don't hesitate to use the elements in this design to decorate your tree with your embroidery!

## Make a Christmas Stocking Ornament

Materials:
- Green, red, and white felt
- Scissors
- White paper
- Pencil
- Glue
- Green, red, and white thread
- Needle

Draw a stocking shape on the white paper. Draw a rectangle the same width; this will be the folded-over top "cuff" of your stocking. Cut them out to use as patterns.

Pin the patterns to the green felt and cut out the two shapes. Repeat using the red felt.

Pin each rectangle onto the top of each stocking shape, aligning the top edges. Sew along the top edge only of each set.

Unfold the flaps and place the two stocking shapes right sides together. Sew around the outside edge, leaving the top edge open. Turn the stocking inside out and fold down the flaps to form the cuff.

Draw snowflakes on the white felt to decorate your stocking. Cut them out and glue them to one side of the stocking.

# Christmas Stocking

Hung at the fireplace mantel,
this homemade stocking will delight both adults and children!

*Instructions on page 92.*

# Dreaming of Toys

A rocking horse, a cradle, a doll, and other toys float
through the sweet dreams of the children in this design.
Your skeins and your needles will carry you away to
the land of imagination . . .

# Tree of Treats

Can you smell all the good Christmas odors? Gingerbread, calissons (a traditional French candy), candy canes, and chocolate Yule logs will come and entice your senses, thanks to this tree of sweets and delicacies.

## THE THIRTEEN CHRISTMAS DESSERTS

While the *bûche de Noël*—the Yule log cake—is an important Christmas dessert in all of France, in Provence another tradition exists: the thirteen Christmas desserts. The number 13 corresponds to the number of people present at the Last Supper. These desserts are served after the famous Christmas dinner. You will find:

**The Four Beggars:**

Walnuts or hazelnuts (to symbolize the Augustines)

Dried figs (to symbolize the Franciscans)

Almonds (to symbolize the Carmelites)

Raisins (to symbolize the Dominicans)

*Pompes à l'huile* or *fougasse* (sweet cake or brioche made with orange-flower water and olive oil)

Soft or brittle nougat

Calissons d'Aix-en-Provence

**The Fruits:**

Green grapes

Oranges or clementines

Candied fruit

Winter apples and pears

Prunes or dates

Dried figs

# Christmas Eve

Tonight, it's certain, Father Christmas will be starting his deliveries, going from house to house to leave a pile of presents under the tree. The children, who are behaving themselves, gaze at the sky for a glimpse of Santa's flying sleigh, then they hang up their stockings.

## Douce Nuit

This carol, sung to the tune of "Silent Night," is one that many French families enjoy. Here is one of the many versions of the lyrics.

| | |
|---|---|
| Douce nuit, blanche nuit, | Sweet night, white night, |
| C'est Noël aujourd'hui | It's Christmas today |
| Et pendant que tes clochers joyeux | And while your happy bells |
| Carillonnent à la voûte des cieux, | Ring out in the vault of heaven, |
| Sous le toit des chaumières | Under the roof of our home |
| On a le cœur bien heureux. | We have a happy heart. |
| | |
| C'est si joli un sapin vert | The green tree is so pretty |
| Qui sourit les bras couverts | Smiling, with covered arms, |
| De lumières et de cheveux d'argent, | Lights, and silver hair, |
| Près du feu qui s'éteint doucement, | Near the fire that's slowly going out |
| Il apporta tant de joies, Lui, | He brought so many joys, He, |
| Le soir où il descendit. | The night He came to Earth. |
| | |
| Douce nuit, blanche nuit, | Sweet night, white night, |
| C'est Noël aujourd'hui, | It's Christmas today, |
| Lui, dans le froid et le vent, | He, in the cold and the wind, |
| Attendu depuis la nuit des temps, | Expected since the beginning of time, |
| Pour nous donner en rêve | To give us a dream |
| Un peu de son paradis. | A little of his paradise |
| À Noël. | At Christmas. |

# Christmas Morning

The long-awaited morning has finally arrived and the promise of lots of presents has been kept. This design shows eyes full of stars and faces lit up with joy, and the warm colors of the Christmases of our childhood.

## Petit Papa Noël
A song known to French children far and wide!

Petit papa Noël
Quand tu descendras du ciel,
Avec des jouets par milliers,
N'oublie pas mon petit soulier.

Mais avant de partir,
Il faudra bien te couvrir,
Dehors tu vas avoir si froid,
C'est un peu à cause de moi.

Il me tarde tant que le jour se lève
Pour voir si tu m'as apporté,
Tous les beaux joujoux que je vois en rêve
Et que je t'ai commandés.

Dear Santa
When you come down from the sky
With thousands of toys
Please don't forget my little stocking.

But before you leave,
Wrap yourself up warmly,
Or you'll catch cold outside,
And it would be my fault.

I'm anxious for morning to come
To see if you have brought me
All the beautiful toys I've been dreaming of
And that I asked you for.

# Advent Calendar

All the previous stitching patterns have a nice surprise in store for you now: you can embroider little bags with each day's number design to create a wonderful advent calendar.

*Instructions on page 94.*

# Christmas ABC Sampler

Finish the festive period in an artistic way by embroidering this sampler full of Christmas spirit. Take time to embroider a complete alphabet, or simply choose the letters of a name or even a message.

# Merry Christmas!

Holly, a little red and green . . . You're ready to wish your family and friends a merry Christmas . . . in cross stitch!

# Happy New Year!

A little mistletoe, sweet surprises, and good will—your family and friends will be delighted with these little stitched wishes while the year changes.

BONNES
FÊTES

BONNES
FÊTES

BONNE
ANNÉE

joyeuses
fêtes

# Greeting Cards

"Merry Christmas!" "Happy New Year!" How about embroidering your greeting cards this year? They'll be more original than a traditional card and warmer than a text message, so send your handmade creations to your family and friends.

*Instructions on page 95.*

The Patterns

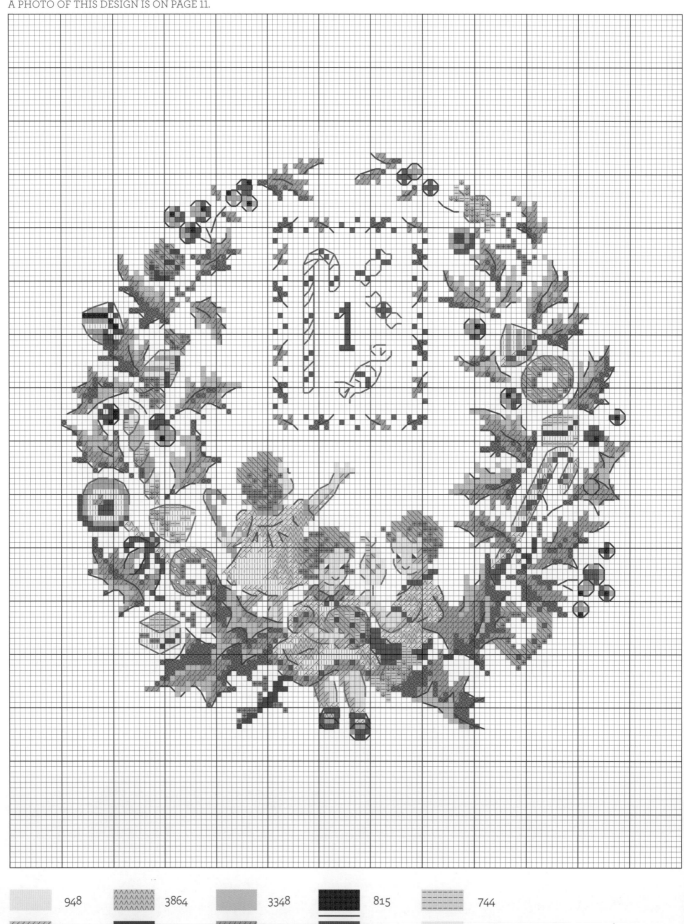

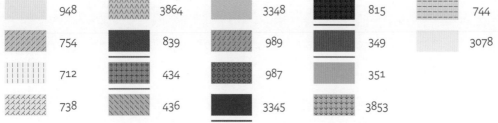

| | | | | | | | | | |
|---|---|---|---|---|---|---|---|---|---|
| | 948 | | 3864 | | 3348 | | 815 | | 744 |
| | 754 | | 839 | | 989 | | 349 | | 3078 |
| | 712 | | 434 | | 987 | | 351 | | |
| | 738 | | 436 | | 3345 | | 3853 | | |

| | 948 | | White | | 747 |
|---|---|---|---|---|---|
| | 754 | | 801 | | 989 | | 815 | | 3766 |
| | 712 | | 434 | | 987 | | 349 | | 3810 |
| | 739 | | 436 | | 3345 | | 351 | | 930 |

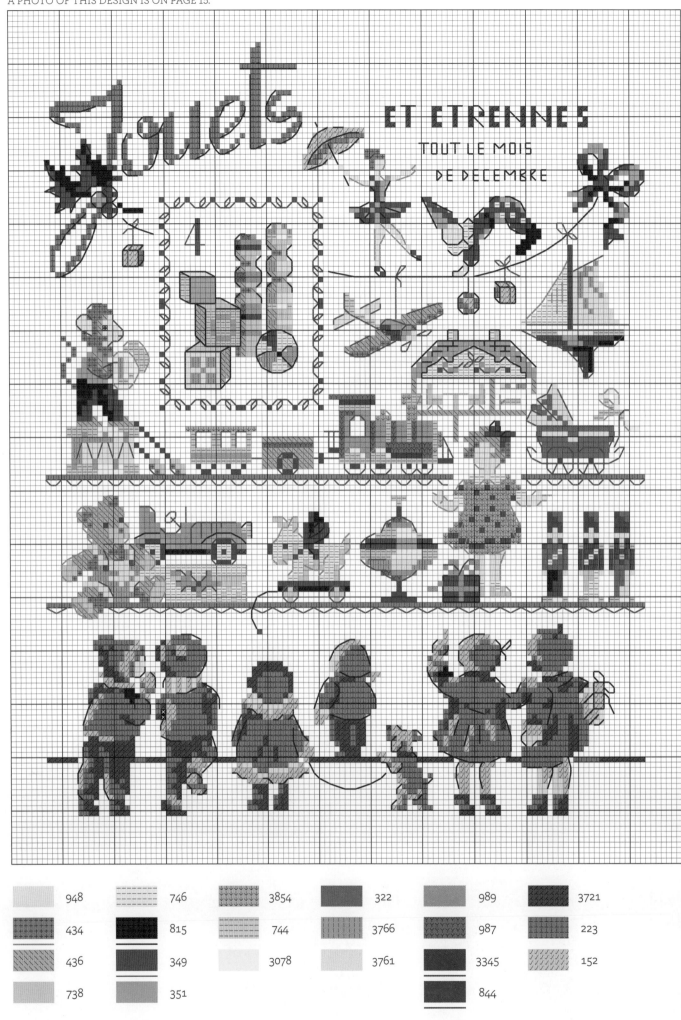

| | | | | | | | | | | |
|---|---|---|---|---|---|---|---|---|---|---|
| | 948 | | 746 | | 3854 | | 322 | | 989 | | 3721 |
| | 434 | | 815 | | 744 | | 3766 | | 987 | | 223 |
| | 436 | | 349 | | 3078 | | 3761 | | 3345 | | 152 |
| | 738 | | 351 | | | | | | 844 | | |

| | 948 | | 801 | | 815 | | 989 | | 3810 | | 168 |
|---|---|---|---|---|---|---|---|---|---|---|---|
| | 754 | | 434 | | 349 | | 987 | | 3766 | | 169 |
| | 712 | | 436 | | 351 | | 3345 | | 747 | | 535 |
| | 739 | | | | | | | | White | | 169 ½ stitch 1 strand |

65

| | 948 | | 739 | | 801 | | 989 | | White | | 169 ½ stitch 1 strand |
| | 754 | | 437 | | 815 | | 987 | | 168 | | |
| | 3078 | | 436 | | 349 | | 3810 | | 169 | | |
| | 744 | | 434 | | 351 | | 3766 | | 535 | | |

| | 948 | | 801 | | 815 | | 3348 | | 3810 |
|---|---|---|---|---|---|---|---|---|---|
| | 754 | | 434 | | 349 | | 989 | | 3766 |
| | 712 | | 436 | | 564 | | 987 | | 747 |
| | 739 | | | | 3816 | | 3345 | | White |

| | 948 | | 712 | | 815 | | 989 | | 747 | | 801 |
| | 754 | | 738 | | 349 | | 987 | | White | | 3345 |
| | 3078 | | 436 | | 351 | | 3810 | | 168 | | |
| | 744 | | 434 | | 3348 | | 3766 | | 535 | | |

| | 948 | | 3864 | | 989 | | 815 | | 3810 |
|---|---|---|---|---|---|---|---|---|---|
| | 754 | | 839 | | 987 | | 349 | | 3766 |
| | White | | 434 | | 744 | | 351 | | 747 |
| | 739 | | 436 | | 3078 | | 3853 | | 3345 |

| | 434 | | 815 | | 3348 | | 564 |
|---|---|---|---|---|---|---|---|
| | 436 | | 349 | | 989 | | 3810 |
| | 738 | | 351 | | 987 | | 3766 |
| | 739 | | 712 | | 3816 | | 747 |

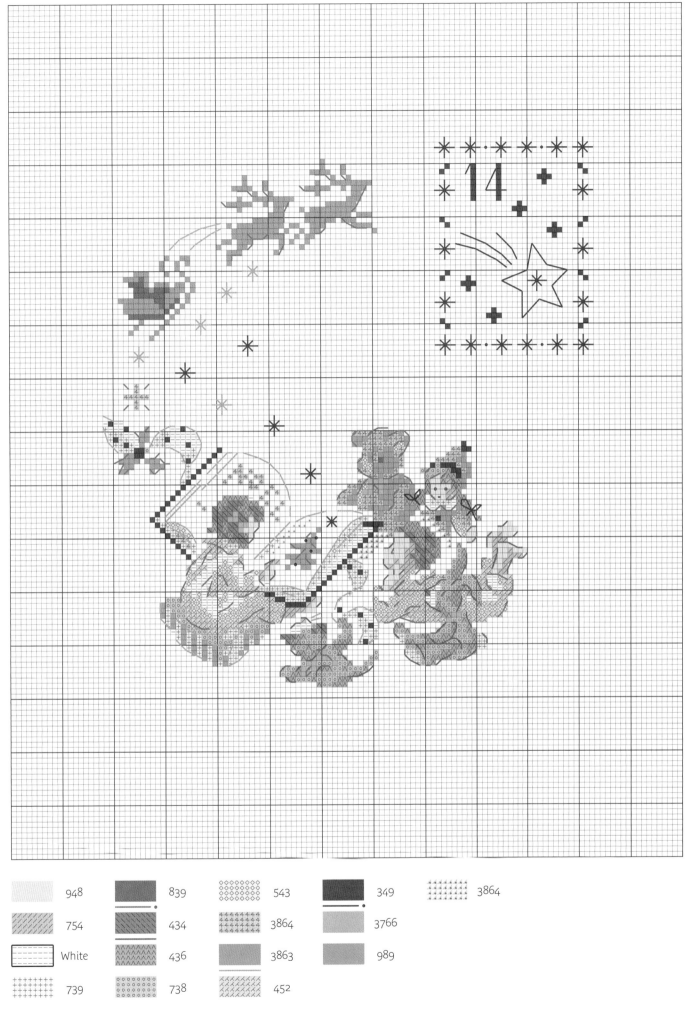

| | | | | | | | | |
|---|---|---|---|---|---|---|---|---|
| | 948 | | 839 | | 543 | | 349 | 3864 |
| | 754 | | 434 | | 3864 | | 3766 | |
| | White | | 436 | | 3863 | | 989 | |
| | 739 | | 738 | | 452 | | | |

| | 754 | | 801 | | 815 | | 989 | | 3766 |
| | 712 | | 434 | | 349 | | 987 | | 747 |
| | 3864 | | 436 | | 351 | | 3345 | | White |
| | 3863 | | 738 | | 744 | | | | |

| | 948 | | 801 | | 815 | | 989 | | 334 |
|---|---|---|---|---|---|---|---|---|---|
| | 754 | | 434 | | 349 | | 987 | | 930 |
| | 712 | | 728 | | 351 | | 561 | | 3810 |
| | 738 | | 744 | | | | 3816 | | 3766 |
| | White | | 3078 | | | | 564 | | 747 |

| | | | | | | | | | | | |
|---|---|---|---|---|---|---|---|---|---|---|---|
| | 801 | | 815 | | 3348 | | White | | 169 |
| | 435 | | 349 | | 989 | | 168 |
| | 437 | | 351 | | 987 | | 169 |
| | 739 | | 3345 | | 535 |

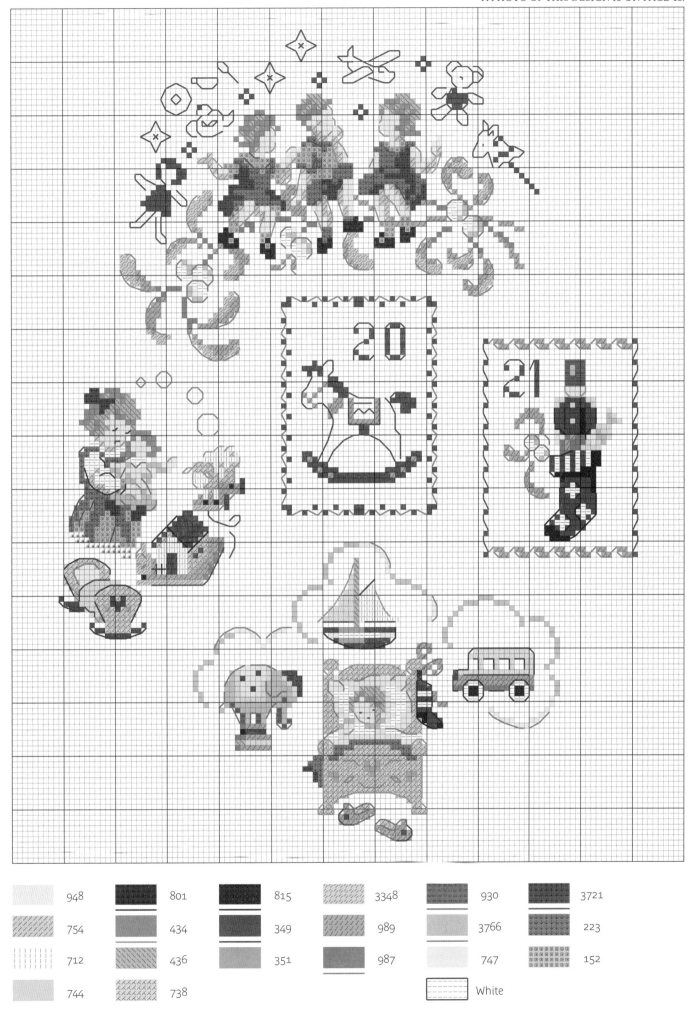

| | 948 | | 801 | | 815 | | 3348 | | 930 | | 3721 |
|---|---|---|---|---|---|---|---|---|---|---|---|
| | 754 | | 434 | | 349 | | 989 | | 3766 | | 223 |
| | 712 | | 436 | | 351 | | 987 | | 747 | | 152 |
| | 744 | | 738 | | | | | | White | | |

| | 801 | | White | | 815 | | 744 | | 3348 | | 168 |
|---|---|---|---|---|---|---|---|---|---|---|---|
| | 434 | | 712 | | 349 | | 3078 | | 989 | | |
| | 436 | | 3864 | | 351 | | 605 | | 987 | | 535 |
| | 738 | | 3863 | | 3853 | | 603 | | 3345 | | |

| | 948 | | 839 | | 815 | | 989 | | 739 |
| --- | --- | --- | --- | --- | --- | --- | --- | --- | --- |
| | 754 | | 434 | | 349 | | 987 | | White |
| | 3864 | | 436 | | 351 | | 3810 | | 168 |
| | 3863 | | 744 | | 3864 | | 3766 | | 535 |

77

| | | | | | | | | | | | |
|---|---|---|---|---|---|---|---|---|---|---|---|
| 948 | | 839 | | 815 | | 3348 | | 535 | | White |
| 754 | | 434 | | 349 | | 989 | | 3810 | | 739 |
| 603 | | 436 | | 351 | | 987 | | 3766 | | 3864 |
| | | 744 | | 3854 | | 3345 | | 747 | | |

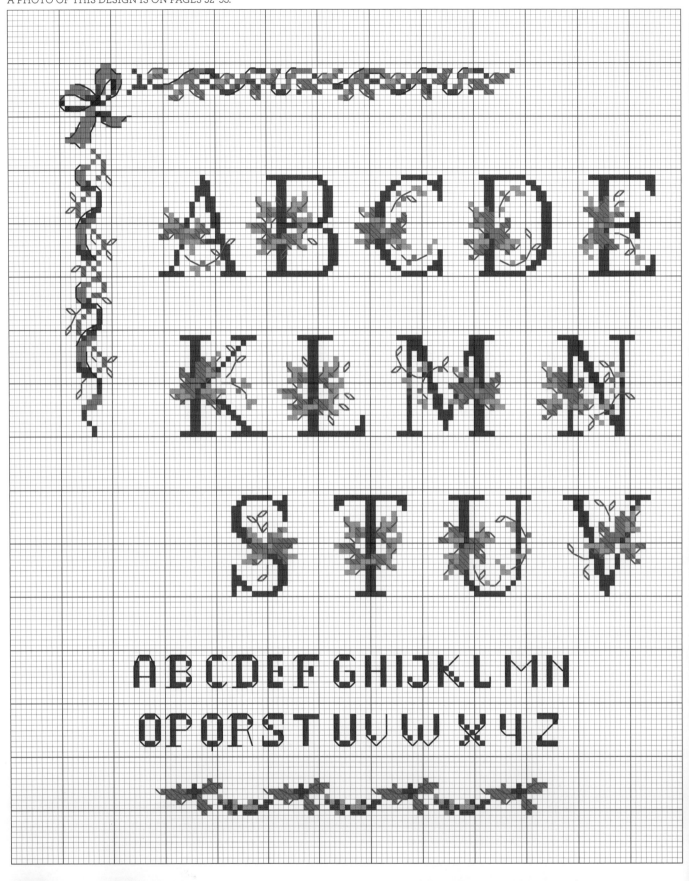

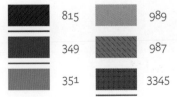

| | 948 | | 839 | | 815 | | 989 | | 3816 |
| | 754 | | 434 | | 349 | | 987 | | 564 |
| | 739 | | 436 | | 351 | | 3345 | | |
| | 3864 | | White | | | | | | |

Techniques & Tips

Cross stitch is easy. It's composed of two crossing slanted stitches. They can be done individually or continuously (see the diagram below).

When doing individual cross stitches, always finish one before starting on another. Your work will be more even.

The best type of thread for cross stitch is called floss. Made up of six cotton strands, it can be divided into fewer strands depending on the fabric's mesh size and the needs of the design. On each pattern, you'll see the color numbers for DMC brand cotton floss.

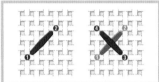

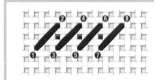

Individual cross stitch

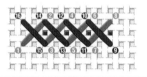

Continuous cross stitch

## OTHER STITCHES

The half cross stitch, or tapestry stitch, is nothing more than a cross stitch with only one slanting stitch. It allows you to reduce the intensity of a color and to create shadow on a background.

The quarter cross stitch lets you create details that are impossible to do with a cross stitch.

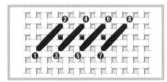

Half cross stitch or
tapestry stitch

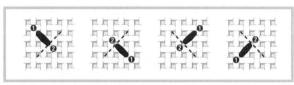

Quarter cross stitch

The three-quarter cross stitch is made up of a half stitch and a quarter stitch. It too helps with adding detail, including curves, to designs.

All three of these stitches are symbolized on the chart in the same way: with a half-square. ◤, ◥, ◣, ◢. It's up to you to choose the type of stitch that works best for the situation.

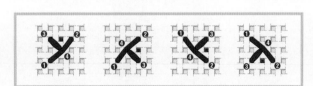

Three-quarter cross stitch

The back stitch, also called the straight stitch, is ideal for bordering a motif, underlining a certain part, or showing a detail, just the way a line drawn with a pencil would. It is done after the entire cross stitch design is completely finished. Usually the back stitch is done with fewer strands than the cross stitch, and most of the time in a color that's a shade darker. Depending on what result you want, you can follow the contours of the crosses, lengthen the stitches, or work diagonally. On the charts, the back stitches are represented by continuous lines.

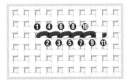

Back stitching on each thread of the canvas

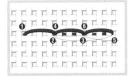

Long back stitch

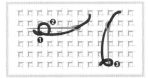

French knot

The French knot is used, for example, for a character's eyes or a flower's stamens, where a cross would be too big. It is indicated on the charts with a small circle ●.

## NEEDLE

The tapestry needle is used for cross stitching. It has a rounded tip, and the eye is larger than a sewing needle's. Its rounded tip helps avoid damage to the canvas mesh, and the larger eye allows for the threading of thicker or multiple strands. The most-common sizes are numbered 18 to 28. The higher the size number, the thinner the needle. A size 26 needle is perfect for working with one strand, but you will need a size 24 needle when working with two or three strands. The mesh size you're working with also helps determine the best needle size.

## EMBROIDERY HOOP

When you are working on a canvas that's not very stiff, you will sometimes need an embroidery hoop. This will keep the canvas taut and keep your stitches even.

## SCISSORS

Use small, pointed scissors and keep them especially for your embroidery. If you carry your work around with you, be careful to keep the scissors away from the canvas to avoid making holes in it.

## FLOSS

All the examples in this book were made using DMC floss; DMC has a range of around 500 colors so you will find the necessary shades for your work.

Floss is made up of six strands that are easy to separate.

Don't lose the color reference numbers of the flosses you are working with. Keep a note of them so that you can find the same shades again.

The size of your finished work depends on the fabric you choose. The fewer stitches it has per inch, the larger your cross stitched work of art will measure.

## AIDA CLOTH

Aida cloth is easy to use. The intercrossing of the threads forms even squares, and each square has defined holes in each corner. Aida cloth comes in various sizes, such as 14 count, 16 count, and 18 count. The size indicates the number of holes, or stitches, per inch.

## LINEN AND OTHER EVENWEAVE FABRICS

Linen is another option. The most-common linen fabrics for cross stitch are 28 count or 32 count. Yes, that means linen has about double the number of holes as Aida cloth, but usually when stitching on linen you do not make a cross stitch on every "square" of the fabric. You skip some holes. On 28-count linen, you might skip one hole per stitch. That would equate to working on 14-count Aida cloth.

Evenweave is the term used to describe other fabrics that have an even warp and weft. Typically, evenweave fabrics are smoother than Aida or linen because they contain some man-made fibers.

Once you have chosen your fabric, cut out a piece that's the size you have determined you need. Remember that the piece should be large enough to allow you to embroider easily. It should also have a sufficient margin on each side to allow for framing or to assemble it in another way (for example, in the projects in the next section).

Oversew the piece to keep the edges from fraying.

Determine the center of the fabric by folding it in four. When working on complex patterns, such as large scenes, tack in a line of thread horizontally and vertically passing through the center of the fabric to guide you. Make sure you don't tack too tightly because you need to be able to remove the tacking easily once you have finished your embroidery.

## Santa's Sack *(photo, pages 18–19)*

Dimensions: 10¾" × 23½"

**Materials:**

White or ecru-colored linen, 27½ threads/in., 22" × 24"

Pom-pom braid, 24" long

Ribbon, 22" long

1. Embroider your chosen designs on the fabric.

2. Fold the fabric in half and align the 22" sides. Sew the sides together ¼" from the edge (diagram 1). Center the seam and sew across the bottom (diagram 2).

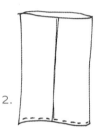

3. Make the corners by centering the bottom seam. Measuring 1½" from each point, sew a line across (diagram 3).

4. Turn the sack right side out and sew the pom-pom braid around the opening. Then fold the ribbon over the edge and sew it in place (diagrams 4 & 5).

# Christmas Tree Ornaments *(photos, pages 30–31)*

## Round Ornament with White Lace
Dimensions: 4" × 4"

**Materials:**
> White or ecru-colored linen, 27½ threads/in., 4" × 4"
>
> Cloth for the back of the ornament, 4" × 4"
>
> Lace, 12" long
>
> Ribbon, 8" long
>
> Fiberfill stuffing

1. Embroider the design on a 4" circle. Cut a circle the same size from the backing cloth.

2. Place the lace along the edge, facing inward, and tack it on (diagram 1). Cover it with the backing. Sew around the circle ¼" from the edge, leaving an opening of 1¾" (diagram 2). Turn it right side out and stuff it (diagram 3). Sew up the opening with small stitches. Sew a ribbon bow onto the back of the ornament (diagram 4).

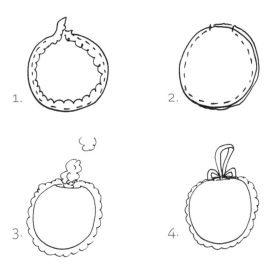

## Heart-Shaped Ornament
Dimensions: 7" × 7"

**Materials:**
> White or ecru-colored linen, 27½ threads/in., 8" × 8"
>
> Cloth for the back of the ornament, 8" × 8"
>
> Braid, 24" long
>
> Ribbon, 8" long
>
> Fiberfill stuffing

Embroider the design and cut out a heart shape around it. Cut a heart the same size from the backing cloth. Put the two pieces together and sew them together ¼" from the edge, leaving an opening of 1¾". Turn it right side out and stuff it. Sew up the opening with small stitches. Sew the braid along the edge of the heart, and sew a ribbon bow onto the back of the ornament.

# Christmas Stocking *(photo, pages 40-41)*

Dimensions: 11" × 19¾"

**Materials:**

White linen, 27½ threads/in., 7½" × 15½"

White cotton cloth for lining, 7½" × 15½"

White synthetic fur, 3¾" × 15½"

Red cloth, 24" × 44"

Ribbon, 11" long

1. Embroider the design, centering it on one half of the 15½" length of the rectangle and leaving ¾" margin at the top and bottom of the design.

2. Cut out a band of fur 3¾" × 15½". Fold it in half lengthwise. Place the cut edges along the bottom of the embroidery and tack it in place (diagram 1).

3. Place the lining on the embroidery, right sides together, and sew along the bottom (diagram 2).

4. Unfold, and fold the piece in half, with the embroidery inside (diagram 3). Sew the side. Turn it right side out and tack the edges that haven't been sewn together. Place the ends of the doubled ribbon along the seam and hand-stitch it on (diagram 4).

5. Enlarge the stocking pattern by 50 percent and cut out two pieces from the red cloth. Assemble the two sides of the stocking and sew them together (diagram 5).

6. Place the fur cuff over the top of the stocking, its right side against the wrong side of stocking. Sew along the top edge (diagram 6). Turn the stocking right side out (diagram 7).

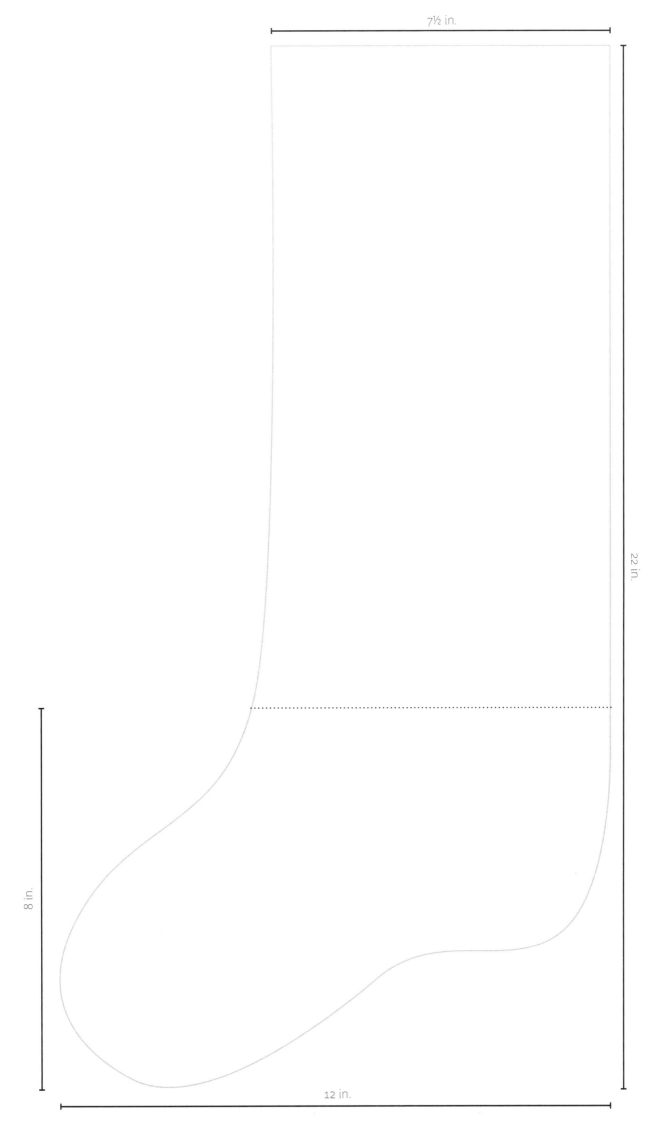

7½ in.

22 in.

8 in.

12 in.

# Advent Calendar *(photos, pages 50–51)*

Dimensions of each bag: 3" × 4"

**Materials:**

    For each of the 24 bags:

    White or ecru-colored linen, 27½ threads/in., 5½" × 7"

    Pearl cotton embroidery floss

1. With each embroidered motif centered on the rectangle, cut the fabric to the above size for each one of the twenty-four bags.

2. Fold the fabric in half, aligning the short sides (diagram 1). Sew at ¼" from the edge, and then center the seam and sew the bottom (diagram 2). Make the corners by centering the bottom seam. Measuring 1½" from each point, sew a line across (diagram 3).

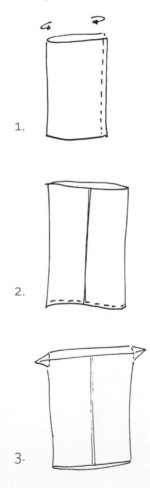

3. Turn each bag right side out; fold the top edge ¼" to the inside. Sew a hanging loop of pearl cotton floss at the center of the back.

# Greeting Cards *(photo, pages 58-59)*

## Envelope

Dimensions: 4¾" × 7½"

**Materials:**

> White linen, 27½ threads/in. (DMC 3865), 8" × 9¾"
>
> White cotton, 8" × 9¾"
>
> Tassel

1. Embroider the design on the fabric, leaving ¾" margin at the bottom of the design. Cut out the shape of the envelope, cutting the bottom angles as shown in the sketch (diagram 1).

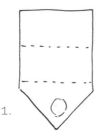

2. Cover with the cotton fabric cut out to the same dimensions, right sides together. Sew ¼" from the edge, leaving a small opening at the top (diagram 2). Turn right side out and sew up the opening. Use an iron to press two folds at the locations shown in diagram 1. Overstitch the sides (diagram 3). Sew on the tassel.

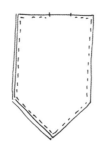

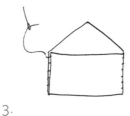

## Card

Dimensions: 4¾" × 4¾"

**Materials:**

> White linen, 27½ threads/in., 8" × 15¾"
>
> Cotton, 8" × 15¾"
>
> Gold lace, 15¾" long
>
> Ribbon, 19" long

1. Embroider the design on the fabric. Fold the edges under and press to finish the edges.

2. Pin the lace along the long edges, facing inward. Cut the ribbon in half and pin a ribbon end at the center of each short sides. Cover with the cotton fabric cut to the same dimensions. Sew around ¼" from the edges, leaving an opening at the top. Turn right side out and sew up the opening.

Illustrator **VÉRONIQUE ENGINGER** is the author of several other books of cross stitch patterns, including *Retro Cross Stitch* and *Fables & Fairy Tales to Cross Stitch*. Her designs often focus on helping the charm of our memories enrich our current-day lives.